PRELIMINARY
VISIONS

KARINA LUTZ

PRELIMINARY VISIONS

POEMS

Homebound Publications

Ensuring the mainstream isn't the only stream

Postal Box 1442, Pawcatuck, Connecticut 06379-1442

WWW.HOMEBOUNDPUBLICATIONS.COM

Quantity sales. Special discounts are available on quantity purchases
by corporations, associations, bookstores and others. For details, contact
the publisher or visit wholesalers such as Ingram or Baker & Taylor.

PAPERBACK ISBN • 9781947003750
Front Cover Image © Diana Parkhouse

Cover and Interior Designed by Leslie M. Browning

Printed in the United States of America
10 9 8 7 6 5 4 3 2 1

Homebound Publications is committed to ecological stewardship.
We greatly value the natural environment and invest in environmental conservation.

CONTENTS

LISTENING

an open window
       a tree
the sound of a man typing
music of a bamboo flute

a woman with closed eyes, sitting

through an open window
       a tree
       in a forest
       one tree

the man stops to eat
the woman stops to think
the tree goes on listening

NEW KINDS OF WEATHER

'Thunder snow' shocks softly
with lavender lightning.
Silence.   Rumbling,
muffling.   Flashes
from high in the low clouds
curiously hard to distinguish from
the arcing of transformers
where wind strains wires
from poles; but those
light the blizzard
from within
with a pale version of new-maple-leaf-&-flower
(lavender's chartreuse)—
                            then all
falls back to grey
                    and greyer.

Indoors, lights flicker
as neighborhood after neighborhood
goes dark all over town,
one side of the street, then ours.
We light dusty candles and
remember how to trim
an oil-lamp wick, pile food from fridge

into coolers on the deck.
Overnight two feet of snow
thrown over them like a lumpy comforter:
moguls of the flatlands;
and we are happy to be homebound.

Finally, as we shovel together,
a chance to talk with the Mormon neighbors
who declined the move-in pie.
That and snowshoeing and the glee
of sledders make a short day
with an excuse to visit the widows
and the divorced.

That evening, a single elder carries
his sleeping bag across the street,
miner's light on his forehead
beaming both ways
—no cars, still white—

and he, a one-time chemist, explains to us
old hippies why he hoped
we might have a hand grinder
for his coffee beans.

AT WILLOW POINT

Not a bird, who would be
able to fly away if the ground turned liquid
below its feet, but something loping,
mammalian, has crossed the rarely frozen cove
since the last snow turned it from silver
to white—Though really,
this color that is said to contain all colors
only to look like their absence
is this evening a greyed lavender,
a muteness under a birdless sky;
it is snow swept flat, reflecting the great, color-field sky's
last moment,
yet brighter—whiter—

And I wish I had ears like the fox
to lead me across with the same
effortless care, hearing each crease
under the skim coat of snow,
with padded bare feet to feel any softness unseen.
I, too, would make a straight course to the island
we usually only visit in summer,
sailing, tacking.

CROWS

You won't go far today
without snowshoes.
It's a day to walk noisily.
The cleats screech against ice—
two feet of snow encrusted
with two inches of ice.
No matter.
It's too cold for anyone but the crows anyway.
So join them, be raucous,
be still and
watch them soar—
and even then, cry out to be heard.

TOE IN

It's not just his shoes.
Here are his skates.
Filling them means putting on the old steel-toed boots
the night before, grabbing a shovel, and
heading down to the pond to clear snow off the ice.
If it's going to be cold enough overnight
you can use that snow to dam the out-stream
with a berm just high enough
to let the water rise
over the bumps in the ice.

Back inside, feed the fire in the stove,
and set the wet socks and boots to dry nearby.
Next morning, pencil the angle of the sunrise
on the window sill and date it,
check the indoor/outdoor thermometer,
make a fresh fire.
Step feet back in warm socks and stiff leather,
and test if the pond's new surface is frozen solid.

To fill his skates means to leave them at the bottom
of the ragged cardboard box,
to follow your kids
as they wobble towards the pond on theirs.

Broad-faced smile
alternating with stern warning,
watch the kids glide,
but keep tracing the edge of the ice
with one toe.

WINTER SOLSTICE LIGHT

Light is like the sun;
As night-blind as earth, we know
light by its absence.

Illumination
we know in gradation:
imperceptible dawn.

We never fully
see the light, like the sun, just
study its contrasts,

stare into shadows.
Yet we hold light's heat through cold
night, remembering.

Illumination
we know through time's gradation:
the thinning of clouds.

Fresh snow like a moon
reflects this muted sunlight
brighter than grey sky.

Wind wipes clouds away
gradually or suddenly:
illumination!

SUN AT SUMMER SOLSTICE

"Abundance! Be like the sun at midday."
—*I Ching*
(trans. Wilhelm/Baynes)

Life is like the sun:
the eye can't look straight at it,
only see its effects.

Illumination
we know in dawn's gradation:
striated purples.

Stars blaze in huge space;
separate in time, yet light
touches another.

Illumined, graded
sunlight reveals a rainbow
where drizzle looked grey.

Made of sun and earth,
life dons a prism of chakras,
and radiates.

Illumination
in gradation, the thinnest
of clouds disappear.

Gradually, or
suddenly—we come to see
sun at solstice noon.

IN LIME ROCK PRESERVE

Extra mothers to each others' kids,
you and I have walked this land
of sweet soil before. Remember: we found
a jack-in-the-pulpit growing here
like an old friend with whom time
collapses to nothing: the joy!

And once we came when the wild dogwoods
floated their white sepals amid
the blooming maples, as if they came
from the same tree.
Though it was named after the calcium
that makes its soil so sweet,
our children had remembered Lime Rock for its clay.
So we brought them back to the streambank,
to where the water carves miniature canyons,
to dig and to play.

Today, as we walk through fall rain without them,
we talk about our aging bones, how acid leaches
the sweetness from them, how the calcium deposits
itself in the wrong places—bone spur, kidney stones.
How it might be that all we have to do is

walk tall and straight for the calcium to know
where to go to rebuild our bones,
as it has been doing all our lives,
our tireless hearts sending it there.

Tireless, like our friendship, our hearts never rest.
How can our hearts need neither rest nor faith to pump
and pump, just some effortless will and grace?

Maybe they rest between each beat—
maybe it is as easy for hearts to keep pumping
as for me to love you, my friend.
You make it so effortless—never failing me, ever,
and always knowing where the deposits are needed,
always seeing, sometimes the obvious
(like I'm moving out after 25 years of marriage
and need a home)
or the invisible (I need someone to reach in
and pull me out of hiding)
or simply to go for a walk,
like when we search this land
for the rare flowers only sweetness grows
(dark crimson lady slippers hidden in leaf mold),
and we mother each other as we wish our mothers had.

And again I will tell you,
again and again until you know it,
how your heart is as sweet as these streams,

as clear to me as these streams,
which carve into the substance of the world,
banking the muddy clay out of which
our children shape their lives.

DOUGH

Our mother baked fresh bread
to the scorn of our classmates
while we knew the secret of its taste,
of its aroma filling the house at the beginning of the afternoon,
of having to wait for the loaves to cool
while temptation pervaded the house—
seethed under doors, distilled in our noses,
condensed in our throats,
dripped to our ready tongues.

"You can't make bread; you have to buy it,"
said one boy, shaking coins of many lands in his pockets.
He would go on to taste
baguette and biscotti,
focaccia, chapatti,
pita, tortilla, and nan,
and plenty of fine wines.
And still today
he doesn't know the feel of dough in his hands,
how it gathers itself to itself,
how it rises and falls and rises again,

how it tastes to wait for it.

TO BE ONE OF WISDOM'S GUESTS

I wanted to be invited in
but all I could do
was peruse the grain of the door,
draw fingertips across the glow of the wood
in the many different lights
of the passing days.

Would age bring me in
passively, inevitably?
Would hard work open wisdom's door?
Would I ever? I am right here, at the stoop,
after all, and seem ready.

Then waiting,
patience turns away from attentiveness
towards the ten thousand things:
the mulberry bushes outside
(who told me they are spiritual medicine?)
and the wisteria framing the door
(isn't love of beauty a path?)
In fact, I make a habit of a haphazard study
        of the infinite paths
to this threshold, where I keep
forgetting why I am here.

And the knocking turns to silence
turns to knocking
and finally, I turn back
to silence.

IN LIGHTNING

In the hills
the sky is not so distant.
The clouds roll low.
On a foggy day we may stand in them,
a world of light surrounding
above and below.
Sometimes the thunderclouds, too, dip
so close the lightning is not a jagged
line but a space...

soft and slow, a pause
of light, while the thunder
starts its rumble almost before the dark falls
again, as it does, so fully,
all moon-, star-, twilight snuffed by the moving clouds
at lightning's end;

then darkfall again pauses—light suspends—
and crashes back down.

(In the hills, it's this darkfall seems harsh,
not the shock of bright light
as in the lowlands.)

We should be afraid, but we're not,
the fat rain its own thunder
and solace.

As we turn our bodies in the dark,
we orient to a new part of the landscape to be illuminated,
to be imprinted,
and carry on in the dark
as the ursine clouds lumber away.

I AM RAINING

My body opens like a flower.
Your hand on my heart sinks to deep center,
surrendering, humbling, elating,
becoming.
With your hand on my breast,
your arm becomes a river,
downstream to me, to you, at once.

I am raining, tiny white flowers
around you,
thousands of petals, floating, flickering,
in this warm light
that is all I am.

AN ATTITUDE OF LISTENING:
A CRAVING

Please
silence me.
Speak to me that way you do, with no words.
Overwhelm my noisy mind
with your huge, hollow heart,
with your enveloping, your echoing,
with your simple, bliss-making smile.

No promises
do I need,
but oh, do I need you
in all your absent glory
in all the mysterious power of your silence,
                    I will surrender.

In solitude I crave:
Please put your finger to my lips.
The silence you touch in me
is love so big my body and soul fall agape
hungry or swallowed
full of emptiness—
We fall as onto a feather bed

to a stillness so deep, it connects us to something infinite

                         —a stillness you awaken

by your presence, your absence,

your immediate and always

and never.

LOOKING (THROUGH LOVE) FORWARD;
LOOKING (FOR LOVE) BACK

"Time goes from present to past."
—Dogen

Remember? We lie in each other's arms
(warmed beside winter's fire)
looking forward
to the new now from the old.

We are now,
then:
this moment when we said:
"imagine the time (shivering in summer's
separation) when we will look
back to these kisses for solace,
for the comfort
so abundant in this present?

"Could any other moment be so fulfilling,
that we won't come back to this?"

"No—" your laugh up my spine—

"Then let's send forward
this bliss."

I am.
I am now that moment:
anticipating this sadness,
and finding its buried fullness.

I am sending forward to now from then, I am
receiving you, as I sit
alone, now, here.

So how are you, my once eternal love?

TRANSCENDENCE/IMMANENCE

I have tasted transcendence—
beyond a holy love, or merging of two souls—
I held infinity, a few moments at a time.

Ordinary life afterwards seemed to be missing
some essential element.
My meditation lately has been to accept
a littler, more circumscribed life.
Seeking that bliss again only makes my
heart sore, like craving an unrequited love,
where devotion itself is almost enough to salve the pain it creates
but not quite.

Trouble is, a habit of loss turns into a habit of fear
and if we're not careful
the desire for communion becomes
a barrier to it.

Again and again I return to my meditation:
to open my heart to the little gifts,
to the mixed pleasures, to what is.

Today there was a light on the grass
for half a moment,
and it meant something—something about
spirit and body,
about what dies with the body
and what may live on with some kind of soul—
The glint, the green flashed an immanence,
and yet it said: no tool
of the mind is sharp enough
to cleave body and soul now,
conceptually, before the fact
of death,

it meant: trying to cleave will elude me,
will be more frustrating, more futile
than sheering passion from love.

All I will be left with is a cleaver—
glinting, flashing, same as the grass,

whispering mysteries.

A GIFT FROM DREAMTIME
for Hannah

"Oh!
I have something beautiful to show you."

Her eyes flicker open closed,
her hand reaches out, heel of palm up,
"see, when you hold it up to the light it sparkles!"

Suddenly, a pull back, a disappointed
"oh" as her empty hand
tucks under her still curled, still waking body.

She doesn't know she has already
given me her gift.

WAKING UP A SIX-YEAR OLD
for Sasha

This sweet, sweet smell
of life itself—I breathe deep draughts
and linger, cheek on softest cheek.
No rush today as I lay my claim to this:
I am here to start her day
and she wakes up happy,
reaches for my neck, flittering eyelashes.
But those tiny butterflies revert to caterpillars,
her eyes moving under lids make the lashes ripple again,
caterpillars climb, fuzzy, slowly as
sleep, one more dream to net in.

Another draught and I thank
whatever it is breathes life into us both.

TETHERS

for Liz, upon her first travels

Tethers of feathers,
light enough to help you fly
Tethers of spun wool,
supple enough to give
Tethers of wholeness,
in spirals to the center of Earth
Tethers of spirit,
stronger than any whirlwind to lift you up
Tethers of green and purple ribbons
winding a maypole
of crocuses and daffodils for you to coast down,
to land to dance again on this sacred ground.

May a circle of arms hold you whole and welcome you home.

FEATHERS

Criss-crossed feathers
push aside cracked eggshell
toward a less muted light.

Wings don't know yet
which way is up.

—the center of this opening—
Only the center
appears
as home,
as bursting,
as too full
for this broken shell.

And now I know
the new light through white
feathers—their spectral edges—
and find new faith
the crosshatch of these wings
across my eyes will emerge
as a pattern   as they unfold.

AS MY FATHER LIES DYING, I GO BY CANOE

"Drive all blames into one."
"Don't be so predictable."
—Tibetan Buddhist lojong precepts

Now I am way lost—
bushwhacking through my husband's unconscious
unskillfully. My anger feels like a machete
would be a fine tool: my hatred applauds the choice
with what little is left of its tiny,
disappearing hands,
as love begins to re-place everything.

Now here I am, being unpredictable, as usual.
Is this how it's supposed to be?
Me flailing against the unknowns
that bind my soul,
against his vegetal restraints,
against the overgrowth of understory,
of love untended for years, all its
untold stories?

I swing at my peril.
Putting down the machete,
I grab fistfuls of these teaching vines
and swing.
           Swinging, swinging,
it's hard to keep my eyes open,
hard to keep them closed.

Now here I am finally tending
the garden of my mother's neglect.
I wade, breathing, through the wild, smothering leaves
of unfamiliar weeds up to my neck,
her dark green depression,
her bilious loss,
her many, many unspoken losses.
I recognize here my husband's neglect,
my own neglect.
I graft these blames into one.

It seems she had planned a covert suicide,
to lose all the losses at once,
as if no one would know—
as if, already buried, no one would notice her dying.
And here now looms finally
the most impossible loss: the divorce she never

felt entitled to, about to be
preempted by her husband's death after all.

Divorce back then
was a forgotten canoe
overturned by the neighbor's shed—
secretly coveted but never asked for,
as she was restrained by a taboo greater
than the one against suicide,
greater than all these wilding weeds;
greater than abuse,
greater than love.

I thrash my way
to the shed
to find the canoe
with one unbroken paddle.

My husband sees behind it
a piece of wood,
a hatchet.

I turn and face the open water.

A GHOST, AN ECHO, ANIMUS

When I dream of you
now that it's over,
a man sings
basso profundo

—the range my waking ears are deaf to hear—

a dirge,
very beautiful,   composed,   true,
nothing from this world,
nor heard before;
no question of putting notes
to page
like you do.

I don't know how
something in me invents this,
something hears this

—song you will never hear—

I don't have that man's
voice, nor do you.
So who is this singing

our ending
as if he knows us?
As if it is this exquisite?

SELF-COUNTERED TRANSFERENCE

A stranger opened the door to the party, not the host.
So I stood with the luck-of-the-pot on a tray, stepped into a space
surrounded by people, everyone else I recognized,
but with the host off in the kitchen,
no one knew what to do with the food.

And right there, right there was my old marriage counselor.
Failed. Both of us. How do we look at each other otherwise?
Hello, do you remember me, my name, assuming he sees hundreds
of us lost souls in the paroxysms of dying marriages,
an EMT of love, saves the few he can
of us lost up our nasty creeks without paddles
and he finds the inner heart more resistant to reawakening
than the outer. And so we both failed,
and moved on and here we are. His wife, I've heard,
has since died of breast cancer. I can't speak of this, either.

How was it we once talked of the most intimate details of my pain,
loss, and fear of the inevitable failure, not inevitable yet,
all that grief and hope tangled?
Like a grandmother helps you prepare a skein of yarn
to wind into a ball, he held his arms out for us
to encircle with the unraveled threads.
My husband-at-the-time even more unable than this man

to get big, round fingertips into those knots.
How I tightened up at his contradiction of my own therapist:
sex is part of the marriage contract, really,
he said. Mine said I needed a break to heal.

Maybe they were both right and that's why I'm here, single
at a party of married folks and teenagers
and this one widower, my own kids off
at some other party with their dad and his sex-willing girlfriend.

Luckily, there are other people to talk to.
Luckily, I don't even wonder until the next morning
if his wife believed, too, that daily, weekly, monthly, or
whatever-it-was-at-the-beginning-divided-by-half
(-by-children, -by-checkbooks, -by-cheese quiches)
some kind of regular sex was required, but she couldn't leave him,
loved him, had no interest in leaving, so had no other choice but
to let the solitude gnawing its way through her breasts
to break through, and to die.
                              But death is not a failure,

it's just life. Begs compassion. So here I am, still alive,
trying not to look him in the eye, while the quiches on the tray
steam up my glasses, coming in from the cold.

CONCENTRIC

"The self is made of nonself elements."
—Thich Nhat Hanh

Our river mouth is midnight still,
an estuary between tides.

Drizzle seeps into mist.

Striding the midline of the dock
to the end, each creak,
each step,
each sway
moves the cry inside
from 'may I
love and be loved'
to
'I love—
        I am love—'

At the end of the dock,
standing still,
see the emergence of slow
ripples, expanding, something like one self
at the center.

WHAT WILL GO DOWN IN MEMORY OF THAT DAY: A CATALOG

looking at your hand holding my hand
as you turn mine over in yours—
twenty-five years dissolve in beauty.

placing a red clover blossom in your mouth
in mid-November, your first
so late in life,

so late in the season,
yet its drupelets of nectar pop open for you
as if it's spring.

speaking your dream aloud, you say the word
"permaculture" as you step, unrecognizing,
through my wild blueberries.

You raise a chant of gratitude,
the new day's blue sky
absorbing your voice.

In these bodies together after all these years
of memories, fantasies, and
ethereal meetings.

standing, your hands on my hips
mine on yours
grounding each other.

I had been afraid of how much I needed
the love you gave unconditionally,
so I turned it down.

I didn't know this as true
until I said it aloud.
next day—you gone—another twenty-five years?—

I shook seeds from evening primrose pods into my hand
and scattered them in the front garden
where the soil is too rocky
for bulbs.

TEN PAPER DARTS AT ONE NEW YEAR'S

I. The poem if you'd left after skating

I flailed at you in skate tag.
How perfect the chase, you
always faster, me always
more passionate,
the ice way too thin at the edges and
bumpy at places—cracking in places.

Fun, fun, fun: pun play as sharp as
the scraping skate blades.
You witnessed your itness—
our breath full and necessary and cheeks red,
bodies warm in the cold,
your smile, your smile,
the inevitable love arising again as my thighs worked,
the sky, white-grey as it prepared to snow,
big and soft enough to hold the love,
the trees around the pond
silent witnesses.

The ice right where I needed it after I hurled myself at
your ever-evasive self and you somehow didn't move,

and my cheek smashed into your shoulder.
I wanted nothing but what was there:
laughter, love, ice, breath, health, warmth,
you, you, you.

You're it.

II. The poem if you had left after the meal

Dharma buddy, I see a pattern.
You attack any new teacher's description of the dharma
with your own. Sometimes it melts down to nothing:
you glimpse emptiness, I see the smile that comes
from that: a smile of ease and satisfaction:
your whole face opens.
Sometimes, your brow twists as your mind binds
thoughts around each other. Sometimes your bullshit detector
gets stuck on like one of those highly sensitive smoke alarms
that need to be moved farther from the kitchen.
Today, in the living room, I loved again
watching you as we conversed
dualism and nondualism,
trying to remember and know one
from the state of the other.

As we often do, we took sides.
We read to each other from
Thich Nhat Hanh's *Teachings on Love.*
How I love your mind, your spirit, how I love being your mirror,
to show you what you can't see of yourself when you're just being
oppositional, like the mirror shows its right hand on your left side,
and any decent friend would hold up her right hand and call it left,
to leave you less confused. We mimed, we talked,
and meanwhile fire burned hidden in the woodstove,
warmed us.

You love to try to figure things out, my friend,
that the mind is inherently incapable of understanding.
And yet, you say, from here, there are the laws of physics.
From here, I say, astrophysicists have spied through scopes
so far back in time that they found an era,
just after the Big Bang, when the laws of physics
did not exist.

Every once in a while, one of us would get up
and peek in the stove,
an eye on the fire.

III. If you had left before the foot massage

My love, I said, please don't drive yet.
The snow is wet on the road,
and the partiers are starting to party.

Yes, you said, but it's only going to get worse.

IV. Up until I said please don't leave me now

You were as beautiful in the twilight
as the giant snowflakes behind you through the window,
floating, hovering, surreally suspended in thick thin air.
It was too lovely to turn on the lights, in a room
with windows in four directions, a space within space
warm inside cold, dark within light.
I lit a candle so I could keep peeking
into your eyes, careful not to stare too long,
one eye on the fire.

You were smiling more. I peeled your socks off, massaged
them with lotion, hands, elbows—going slowly so as to not
beg the questions—you often are happy with just a massage.
Hands, elbows, eyes, listening to your voice,
your laugh as always spinal in me, rippling.

I pulled your feet, pushed them, bent your knee
and leaned in, Thai style, my weight towards your heart,
stretching your legs and back, our happy bellies…
Now what?

Why or why not?
I can't help loving you, you know that, the only question is
what kind of love. Is it always mixed, the unconditional
with the confusion of desire, the errors of attachment?

No.
I returned to my practice, to my breath,
pacing passion by letting it rise and pass again and again,
the stove closed down tightly
though I let in enough air to keep the fire alive,
for a slow, full burn. Steady love beams like radiant heat.

Then you let us kiss.

And once again, we are skating on thin ice.
This is where you usually say goodbye.

But you took me by hand
and led me to bed.

Remembering literally takes my breath away: a big "huh"
spoken on the in-breath and gone.
I feel my womb contract
and the energy hidden there flies up through my core
to my way-too-open heart;
the energy skids the big screechy shush of a sideways skate blade,
gets lost in the trying to let go, gets stuck around the periphery
of my chest, under the collarbones, in the remote corners
of the heart itself.

My love and my passion at odds,
because as soon as you are inside me
you want to stop. I want to honor you but I hear your mind
and spirit and body telling me different things. Passion wins,
I grasp your hipbones.

But you cannot stay.

V. The poem if you'd left without talking it out

I need you to finish pleasuring me. To ask evokes your shame
but your hurt comes out as hurtfulness and I
succumb to that as well.
I don't realize this at the time.
I allow you to shame me, and not until your side

of the bed grows bone cold will my gut say:

I   will   not   be   shamed.

Heart adds: nor will I shame.

VI. What really happened

I was coming up to a peak of passion, had let go the guard,
flown open the woodstove doors,
it was beginning to roar and then,
blocked at the flue,
smoke filled the house,
smudging us with anger, aversion,
and you asked me
to stop feeling pain, desire.
                    I couldn't but stopped asking for more.
Then you asked: please honor
that I don't want sex like you want sex.
Of course your no trumps my yes.
Besides, I want yes-I-said-yes-I-will-Yes abandonment.
You want to teach me to accept No.

The golden rule does not always apply:
true love is not giving what you want to receive

nor what you have handy to give, but what the other needs.
You see this and ask me for what you really want:
for me not to want to change you.

So out with the old. The old dream of healing,
that I could fall back in love a third time (or is it seventh
or eighth by now? Depends on how you count fires:
if there were still enough coals to start new kindling,
was that new? or maybe it doesn't count if you banked the coals).
Here I am, water, water,

stirring the hissing ashes.

Yet I refuse to starve the love its air.
That would mean stopping breathing.
Instead, I will I tease out sex-passion from love,
conditional from un-,
truth from attachment,
aversion from letting
go.

VII. Sleep's koan

No shame,
No blame,
Just change.

VIII. If you had stayed for breakfast

I wake up, recalling your sweat from the night before,
how fine it was, all over you,
how you opened the window, and let the cold
pour all over you, how I'd had to climb
under the covers. I tiptoe past the room
where you slept, see your mouth open,
vulnerable, trusting, keep walking, open the stove, peek in.
Tiny redness peeks back out of the ash-dusted coals.
Snow dusts the trees (still silent),
the fields, the cars, the road.
Pink and blue streak the sky, and where night's wind
already blew off the dusting,
the icy crust on the field shines lavender.
I dust snow off wood, carry it in,
build a new fire. It doesn't need a match.

At breakfast you are smiling again. You are forgiving,
I am forgiving, but we still have
no clue how to love each other well.

I imagine this poem from bed.
Pull the covers to my neck,
too cold to build a new fire.

I hurt like a 17-year-old girl in a 47-year-old body:
losing the same lover again.
I sob my letting go, fully, for good
this time, for real. Out with the old.

IX. If you'd come to the woods for the ritual...

...it would have been very different.
Maybe you would have liked to see
my soul-sister smudge me,
pray for me to let go of the old attachment
to failed love and make room for the new.
Maybe you would have had something else
to say to the goddess, who we invited
to clear our spirits and bring us
new loves and skillful means.

You might have been shocked to see
when the smoke touched me and
my sister's words made it through my mind and through my body
to what had lain asleep in my solar plexus,
how it looked like an orgasm. How I made a similar
sound. How the energy burned up my feet from the snow
and rattled out the crown of my head, how I got it.

I think that was a yes.

X. Another kind of yes

I smudged my sister in the new light of the open sky
above the old maple, which had died and fallen
almost all the way to the ground.
It was easy to pray for her, golden-rule easy,
to wish her what I wished: a new lover, as soon as she is ready,
one who'd love her well and deeply;
that she will know she deserves this,
as she is so loving and giving and ripe;
that spirit fill her: fresh, full, nourishing, clear.

Over by the oldest living maple, where a half-frozen vernal pool
covered the living green of a hardy violet, and a spider
walked across the water, a miracle,
we prayed for all earth:
Clean air, clear water, and plenty of healthy food for all.

I would have loved to wave the lavender and white sage
into your whitening, wild hair,
with the snow on the maple bark behind you.
How the tree would have framed you,
held you in love as it did us.
How the bits of snow alighting from the canopy above

would have moistened your cheek as they melted, cool tears:
how I would have loved you.

But would you have loved the new prayer that keeps singing?
Or would you have imagined we kept the loss at bay, outside
the circle of our snow-lit hope?

Could we have been as open to spirit as we were without you?

And would you have let the goddess shake you free,
would you let her touch you like you had, the night before,
let my fingers at your nape
awaken your spine?

You're it.

DEER PATH

A quiet road
Dirt well packed by tractors
Bicycle lines in the soft parts
Swerving back & forth

The stillness, greyness, black branches straining upward.
A hint of spring promise in a scent on the wind.
Still cold,
bundled and alone.

The alone that loves to be alone,
that breaks away and moves along
a deer path through the birches,
and is fascinated by each red-budded branch tip
and cautious piece of green pushing through
the old wet leaves.

The alone that lingers with sorrow,
that rides the grey clouds to the past,
and loves to yearn;
for the spring, for the past
for a love that was shared
and now is chased away
by the lover of being alone.

MIDWAY THROUGH THE HIKE

They had hiked so long they knew not whether
to take off their boots to save their blisters
or keep them on to save their soles.
Joking of such things had hit a peak three ridges back,
luscious silences ensued.
The colors of forest, boulder field, flower, and sky
imperceptibly grew more rich and lucid,
until a depth of light they'd never before seen
emanated from all objects
within their gaze, whether shadowed or blazing in sunlight—
yet not psychedelic, no movie effects, nothing surreal—
only the realer reality of the simply seen
by the open eyes of a healthy body,
a body fully oxygenated, fully circulating,
its center of gravity slung low and strong
and moving steadily forward.

The three hikers stopped to tend their feet streamside,
splashing, wetting, wringing,
hanging clean socks to dry from the backs of their packs.
They drank water from plastic bottles while longing
for the days of open mouths in streams,
imagined pouring all the dead water out

and returning it to the living, imagined a life without fear or will.
The ambition of their 70-pound packs,
now strewn on the streambank,
seemed suddenly absurd, made them want to get naked,
what the hell, a giddy gratitude began to glimmer up their throats
at the silliness of the ambition that had brought them to this place
and beyond the pain and beyond the tiredness,
beyond the talking and virtually every desire but the desire
to trek the full distance
(and even that they had taken turns talking each other back into).
That gratitude made it safer to undress than to do anything else,
the only sensible thing to do, to bring them
fully here at rest, beside the path,
muscles cooling and toes happily spread
and skin wrapped in the silk of water.

By dusk they found themselves fully alive:
surrendered, unremembering, readying for slumber
in skins as fresh as a pool beside a sweat lodge,
with hearts relentlessly beating,
the way water flows under the apparent stillness of the pool,

destination as yet unknown.

AT BEAVERTAIL POINT

I find
all nature erotic,
you said.

Even rocks.

It was the waves
that whispered in our ears
all day long,
the sun
that pressed,
warm,
then hot.
Breezes
tickled the down
at the back
of your neck,

but rocks?

Yes:
pale orange cliffs
sheltered us from wind,

cupped winter sun,
made it easy
to lounge,
to kiss until
the tide came in.

Below us, unseen
because we could not
unlock eyes from each other,
rocks made pools
to hold anemones
and protected them from the waves
for those languid hours—
anemones
who would have sucked our fingers
into themselves
at the slightest touch.

Bobbing seals sent sidelong glances
from deep, wet eyes.

Above the cliffs,
the wind would make

our nipples erect.
But down below, the rocks surrounded
us and poured us their cup of sunlight,
our sustenance.

All good qualities in a lover.

But all that
anthropomorphizing
dropped away
as will happen
with enough simple being

—the rocks have time,
know stillness—

All nature,
all being, erotic:

an invitation
to connect,

an invitation
to enjoy.

ROCKS

I.

alive

      buzzing molecules

      crystals growing slowly

      edges dying, crumbling into soil

rocks

      becoming again

      from the pressure between

gravity, pulling down

earth, swelling outward

II.

Maybe rocks are running the whole show.

Maybe they have us running around for them

gathering ingredients; mining and grinding quarries,

building foundries to melt metals,

mixing plastics from distillations, concentrations

of elements, from all over this world, gathering

them into what we call landfills;

wombs of new kinds of rocks.

A new oil, the amniotic sac,

releases as consciousness begins to reside

in a new stone, here to develop for millennia,

here to watch the surface change.
Soil clings and is swept away
by the wind, which does little more to the rock
than speed its shedding.

III.
When rocks laugh
we have earthquakes.
It's not that they have anything against us.
They appreciate what we do to them,
it's just that chisels and 'dozers tickle.
They love what we've done with marble,
gravel, graves, like a good jackhammering once in a while.
Don't mind being shaped into Stonehenge, Newgrange,
Machu Pichu, Notre Dame,
sphinxes, pyramids, and pietas,
The Thinker, the David, and many Moore.
If they have no quarrel with the tickling people,
why should we cry when they laugh?

IV.
Who did the rocks have melt down the honey-colored goo
to pour over flies and fossilize in amber?
Who petrified the wood of a whole forest
and froze sand over the fallen logs?

V.

Rocks have places they belong.

Be careful which you choose to move.

Some rocks won't stand for not being returned

where they came from.

Their mountains will move,

burst up, burning spew.

VI.

You don't want to get in the way of a rock.

They aren't forgiving. They don't have to be.

They move of a force that is not their own:

No will, no blame.

ARMY-NAVY SURPLUS

Behind a 100-square-yard sheet of plate glass
        (quite a technological feat in and of itself!)
a display is suspended:
outboard motors, lawn mowers (is that a washing machine?)
—all in camouflage—
hair dryers, river rafts, mountaineering gear.

On each end a mannequin stands,
headless, in uniform
(also camouflage).

How do they get the caps to suspend
like that, in the air, over
where the head should be?

MILES OF BUILDINGS AND TREES

Factories and shipyards interspersed
with patches of trees and salt marsh.
The sun gilds between bluing clouds, water silvers,
lights pop on along roadsides
and one flickers, a fluorescent struggle
above my head.

Someone bangs a suitcase against a seat,
as a crowd quickly fills the aisle,
then pours out on the town.
The capitol building overlooks the station
like a palace or temple, blends its blue-grey
with the sky's.
Dust on the window whitens,
catching light from sinking dusk.
Somewhere a constant ring, hardly audible, is ignored.

Moving again.
An elevated highway, a kinetic skyline,
passes silhouettes of trucks across
the purple-orange sky,
brick buildings flip over it like pages
then rip away.

EQUALLY INVISIBLE

Cancer harvested these ghosts as
children. Out of love,
they haunt. They
   float up
stream,
    fly up
wind,
    fal-
ter and hover

looking in
out
   fall pipes
looking down
smoke
      stacks.

See! A troop of the child ghosts
works under a willow,
weaving the baskets and nets
they will scoop with.

More! Over there in the field!

They scythe away
at the particles,
already too small, too small.
And they are giggling,
like children.

Like children, they reach right out to try
to stop the effluent and emissions,
as if their tiny invisible hands can stop
poisons and radiation.

Water, air
          slip
               through.

Listen carefully, for they will tell you,
you future generations and wild things
(if you exist):

"Watch out here,
this is where the poison lies."

SUPERPOWER

We live in a land where people crunch pre-cut cantaloupes
from plastic cups while running through airports—
no patience for ripening.

We live in a land where adults give children presents of toys
that train them to press the buttons that shoot and bomb
aliens, critters, invaders, anyone else coming towards them.
No time to look.

We live in a land where it is considered a luxury to need a car
to get to day care to get to work to get the car to get back home—
dodging other cars and trucks moving fast enough
to shatter our cocoons of glass and steel—
fast enough to get back home safe and sound.
To rest.

We live so sadly alone we must take pills to keep us from killing
ourselves and other pills to stop fearing death and other pills
to stop our hearts from stopping—pills to help us outlive death.

We live in a land where men in power refusing themselves sex
steal it from children, like their own was stolen from them
as children nobody heard,

when the taboo against speaking about these things
was stronger than the taboo against doing them.

We live in a land where one arm of government passes a law
to take away the right to send a letter unread by spies,
the same year another arm passes a law
to make sure the environmental police must have a warrant
to walk on your land to see if you are robbing people
of clean water, clean air, the right to breathe.

We live in a land that holds the image of a woman
in a burqua in horror,
yet sees the frozen stare of near-naked,
near-starving model-images
as free, as "statuesque."

We live in a land where the idea of saving downtown
is to subsidize a mall, is to use
public money to enclose public functions in private property,
so we can separate shoppers with money
from the hungry and the desperate,
from the men who need alcohol and drugs to stop themselves
from killing themselves or who do it more slowly,
let it ripen in full view of the street.

But the streets are nearly empty now in the shadow of the mall,
the city mall wrapped in a parking garage three times its size,
where shoppers buy plastic-coated plastic
and shove it in plastic shopping bags
in flagrant pseudo-opulence.

We live in fear that someone will take from us
what we have been taking from the world:
Power, wealth, beauty, innocence,
fruit before it is ripe:

our way of life.

LEARNING TO MAKE PEACE

After a day of trailing my mother
from house to house or along the beach
gathering signatures on petitions,
our dinner conversation might start:
What if America had not fought in World War II?
How else can you stop an aggressor like Hitler but with war?

One of us kids saw a way:
What if
the German people had not supported, succumbed, colluded?
What if
the members of the S.S.
had turned toward peace?

It became clearer and clearer,
as did my mother's voice,
that in Vietnam, we Americans
were the perpetrators, the collaborators.

We were the ones with the most power to make peace.

Meanwhile the news came in body counts and draft numbers,
riots, conventions; conventions that turned into riots.

Pacifists demonstrating protests don't have to be riots.
That peace could be deadly fun.
And there was my dad, watching vigorously,
studying, shouting.
Other nights I spied from the top of the stairs, long after bedtime,
the town's Democrats in our living room,
choosing delegates to those conventions
or the League of Women Voters planning a debate.

But the best debate team was there around the kitchen table.
At the head was a man, a good soldier from the Good War,
trying to be the best he could—
so brave and yet so afraid to think any of the wars he had fought
might have been wrong.

Right there was the miracle
of my parents' marriage:
words could make change,
love could make peace.

One day he wrote a letter: the war should be stopped,
Signed, Naval Reserve Captain, our father's name.

Her ten thousand petition signatures,
and his one letter:

a man of violence
turned toward peace
before our eyes.

I have received many gifts from my parents,
But no greater gift than this.

INSIDE JOB

He worked at a nuclear power plant
and secretly hated his work,
though no one was able to tell
(like a serial killer who "seemed like a nice
enough guy, kinda quiet"), certainly not
the guys and wives at the country club,
against whom he always argued defense,
half high, around the small punctuation
of ice in glasses, glasses half empty of the ghost
of juniper and tonic.

              But at some invisible point,
he had half fallen for one of
the hippies at the gate

                he drove past every morning
and evening, as she held vigil with her long, curly hair,
her absurd herbs & feathers to stop
nuclear power & weapons,
as if.

His muttering stopped inaudibly at that point,
like a river-crossing in winter
(the water's movement under a foot of ice),
the solidity silent and shoe-shushed over.

Nothing then was the same, except everything
on the outside. The spent fuel rods still needed
monitoring, as they would for the next eon,
by someone he dared not imagine.

New fuel rods still needed, it seemed, to be lowered
into place, the fail safes engaged,
the protocols observed. But he was able to discover
and plot more reasons to delay the lowering, and
to shut down the plant more often
                              until the profit margin shrank
to a shadow of its former self, and one day, one fine day,
he'd work his way out of the part of the job he grew to hate most,
the loading of fresh fuel, the birth of the next
quasi-eternity, the setting in motion work for future generations,
work that will be for no good at all, just dangerous drudgery,
only to have served power
to the hair dryers and factories and Xboxes
the future's ghosts will have once used, back in their day,

our day.

UPON ASCENDING
INTO THE WORLD TRADE CENTER
(from the subway, early spring, 2000)

Standing stock still as people streamed every way
around her, expertly parting as little as possible
as if she were a mere rock in a river.
Could she be weeping?

She had just trained in for the first time
from her white suburb
to this city of dangers told by radio.
All around her, moving fast: strange
faces, different colors, different voices,
languages she had never heard before.

She rubbed her pockets in a downward motion.
Did she find herself weeping?!?

A tissue offered
by a black hand.
She looked up into a round face
surrounded by a blue-and-orange head wrap,
the darkest skin she'd ever seen,
blacker eyes, as kind as any she'd fallen into:

"Welcome to New York."

MASS MOURNING

Finally,
we cracked.
Poured out into the streets
to mourn the measure of our losses,
flooded houses of worship,
in parks held candleless vigils:
wicks couldn't hold a flame through the driving tears.

A man (he must have heard the news
of this latest senselessness on the radio)
opened the door to his car and let the stored tears
burst into the gutter.

It wasn't the first time we'd wept:
one time, even a President's voice had cracked.
The mothers of pistol fodder,
the police fodder, the invisible until shot,
have been crying since 'emancipation,'
and of course since long before, each time a mate or child stolen,
each time a massacre, a genocide occurred or obscured.
Churches had had cry-ins
at the still-smoldering buildings:
and when firehose water was not enough,
our tears quelled the last of the embers.

In Colombine and Newtown,
we wept in schoolyards.
Jackson State, Kent State, Virginia Tech.
Whole communities:
Aurora and Oklahoma City.
We stopped counting.

Surely individuals, unreported, standing,
had cried into their TVs until they shorted out
one war or another,
having given up pounding the top of the set
with their sore fists.

But this time the dam broke.

Even the color guard snapped,
laid down their rifles, kneeled over them
and cried until they washed away.
The streets were finally, literally
flooded. We couldn't stop mourning.
The anger, the blame—now useless.
The stoicism, the cynicism—stopped.
Eyes widened, then squeezed.

Wailing, like you hear some cultures do at funerals.
Wailing, like cops' sirens, like an ambulance.
This time it wasn't just our own,
it was Beirut and Paris, Syria and Iraq
Iran, Vietnam, Hiroshima, Bosnia
Korea, the Congo, Yugoslavia, Guatemala, Libya,
Guatemala, Libya, again
All the places we have bombed:
Bikini Atoll, and other obscure places whose names
we can't pronounce, places we can't find on a map.

Finally it hits us:
How many have died?
How many loved ones and strangers?
How useless the violence has been!
Children gunned down—motive unclear.
Who to hate? Who to fear?
Children abused,
women and men raped, queers bashed,
all the techniques of torture and terror—
no sense to be made—
no sense.

But this time even the children refused to fear,
just cry.

We all refused to fight back,
for who else was left to attack?

Just cry.

Rivers overflowed and washed through Walmarts.
Guns floated and sank, war games, too.
Warhead silos, rusty already, filled to the brim.
Still we couldn't stop.
We could feel how related we are to all
we had destroyed, we ripped our garments,
tore our callouses off and cried,
it didn't matter anymore, we were all so related,
out in that field beyond right and wrong.

There was a little calm there.
We began to connect,
little smiles of recognition,
our ancient faces, our child faces showing through
the bitter mask of this life.

Then it got worse:
we remembered the species
extinct or nearly.

A woman opened the door to the natural history museum
and the dodo bird
all the taxidermy
horn of black rhino
bones of whale
began to flow out and still float.

Gale winds sprung the zoo and the factory farm gates open
the wailing now howling.
All kinds of eerie voices added in:
the cry of a baby coyote separated from her pack,
the cry of a swan who's lost a mate,
a loon's ancient echo off a lake.

Our sorrow multiplied,
but we carried it for each other.
Our hearts squeezed, throats squeezed
then opened
like a spigot
like a fire hydrant on a hot day
in the city.

We walked through our tears
until we could gather and see each others' faces
washed clean and open

and we listened again
to the sound of the loon
as she landed
on the lake we had made.

WAKE UP!

Wake up! This is a message from
the other life you live, without weariness,
while you sleep.
                    Wake up!
Time to translate. You might use
the hand that you saw with such grain,
such fineness: each line alive

(you could see some depth inside the skin,
a reverse aura, as luminous)…

but you cannot see that hand in front of you now.
This cold morning shows you your old hands,
small, female hands, which somehow inhabit
this same space, but for some reason, when eyes open
the dreamhand is invisible.

Hurry now, while it is still at least present
to translate: reconstruct the images backwards
from the poignant last one and the voice that
called: Awaken!
First remember it as

fragments of a dream sequence,
though your recall is not remotely linear

—one central vision lay thoroughly outside time—

Perhaps the movie ran three times and the
last seen was the director's cut, because you remember
this after that and this doesn't make sense after that.
Then again, he was you, all in one moment,
not like you understand reincarnation,
as your day-mind is comfortable only
with the soul or whatever it is floating
for one month max, then finding a fetus—

No, no there is no "time line"
for this dream, the only lines are rays, radiances, all
connected back to themselves—"simultaneous" does no justice,
"stream of consciousness" still too mind-in-time-bound (the "yes"
Joyce found interjected in the transcription of his dictation,
puzzlingly out-of-place, then remembered to be his own answer
 to a knock on the door
[a mere interruption, the affirmation]
but left in.)

Yes.

CIRCLES

Today a man prepares to start to walk.
He calls out: who will join him?
To encircle earth, to pray with feet,
to love with feet, to touch, to spring.

His feet tingle with all they touch
and he loves all he sees:
and in spite of the despair in so many faces
he sees a world revolving toward peace!
And he is not alone.

At the top of the world lives an elder
who sees the same vision.
I am shaken awake by the same dream:

Walkers spontaneously joining in a stream
and completing a circle around the world,
making real the prayers of eons.

Each finds her place, by moving.
A peacemaking migration,
an artmaking pilgrimage,
each walker carrying medicines to share:
seeds, roots, flowers, stems, fruits.

Monks and nuns have been building pagodas
along a circle around the earth.
An artist builds earth sculptures
along a circumference.
What is left of ancient pilgrims' paths
trace pieces of the circle
under the Milky Way.

Will we make it whole again?

[REFRAIN]

No 'good enough.'
No 'not good enough.'

No shame,
No blame,
Just change.

ACKNOWLEDGMENTS

"An attitude of listening:/a craving" published as "A craving"
   in *The Wayfarer* (Spring 2014): 9.

"At Willow Point," *Clade Song VI* (Summer 2016).

"At Beavertail Point," *S/tick,* 13.2 (Winter 2018): 14.

"As my father lies dying, I go by canoe" was published as "Canoe" in
   the *RavensPerch* (June 5, 2016)

"Concentric," *Written River* V, no. 1 (Summer 2014): 21.

"Deer path," *The Wayfarer* (Spring 2014): 9.

"Dough," S/tick (Winter 2016) 3.2:16.

"Equally invisible," *The Bleeding Lion* no. 2 (Summer 2015) pp. 61.

"I am raining," lyrics for *Songs of Intimacy*, Todd Winkler,
   composer, 1986. Copyright Karina Lutz and Todd Winkler.

"In lightning," *Written River* V, no. 1 (Summer 2014): 21.

"In Lime Rock Preserve," *Poecology* V (Aug. 2015).

"Inside job," *Deep Times: A Journal of the Work That Reconnects*
   (May 2017).

"Mass mourning," *Visitant* (July 7, 2016).

"Midway through the hike," *Green Living Journal* (Fall 2006): 41.

"New kinds of weather," *Shortest Day, Longest Night*, ed.
   Cherry Potts (London: Arachne Press, 2016): 58-9.

"Self-countered transference," *Twisted Vine Literary Arts Journal*
   (Fall 2015): 101.

"Superpower," Opus Terra and E-Scribes websites, 2006.

"Ten paper darts at one New Year's," *Sediments Literary-Arts
   Journal,* (Happy Holidays issue 2016): 11 ff.

"Upon ascending into the World Trade Center," *Echoes of Mercy*
   (anthology), (Newport, RI: Salve Regina University, 2015).

About the Author

Karina Lutz worked as an environmental activist to help secure passage of sustainable energy legislation, thwart a proposed megaport, and restore wetlands in her home watershed of Narragansett Bay, RI. She helped launch a nonprofit green power company and is currently collaborating to form an intentional community, Listening Tree Cooperative, practicing permaculture in northwest Rhode Island. With an MSJ from Medill School of Journalism, she has worked as an editor, reporter, magazine publisher, and in nonprofit communications.

Her chapbook, *Post-Catholic Midrashim*, was published in 2019. Information about her publications can be found at: www.karinalutz. wordpress.com.

HOMEBOUND PUBLICATIONS
POETRY OFFERINGS

———